The Call
and
the Cry

Poets respond to gun violence in America

Deer Dancer Press
P.O. Box 301
Anacortes, WA. 98221 USA
deerdancerpress@gmail.com

In memory of
Nancy Rekow (1932-2023)
and
Cathy Cuenin (1949-2022)

Both knew the power of poetry to inspire and to heal

"The violence causes silence.
We must be mistaken."

From "Zombie" by Delores O'Riordan and The Cranberries

INTRODUCTION

Most of the poems in this book were written in response to the murder of 58 people on Oct. 1, 2017 by a sniper in a hotel room in Las Vegas, Nevada. In addition to those killed, 527 people were injured. The poems were originally published that year under the title "Poems for Las Vegas" (Kitsap Publishing).

Oct. 1, 2017 left the nation grasping to understand how such an atrocity could happen. The poets of "Poems for Las Vegas" produced their thoughtful works to help readers process the tragedy and horror of that day and to provide some measure of comfort.

The violence of that day defied belief. And yet, such violence continues in our country.

In 2018, 322 mass shootings, 387 human beings dead, 1,274 injured.

In 2019, 434 mass shootings, 517 human beings dead, 1,643 injured.

In 2020, 615 mass shootings, 521 human beings dead, 2,541 injured.

In 2021, 693 mass shootings, 703 human beings dead, 2,842 injured.

In 2022, 695 mass shootings, 761 human beings dead, 2,902 injured.

In 2023, 598 mass shootings, 730 human beings dead, 2,440 injured.

Human beings — not statistics. Each carried the breath of life. Each loved and was loved, had a family, attended local schools, worshipped in a local church, worked in his or her community.

The late Sen. Robert F. Kennedy of New York might say, as he did in 1968 during another violent period in our nation's history, that these individuals were "most important of all, human beings whom other human beings loved and needed." And he might remind us now, as he did then, that "No one — no matter where he lives or what he does — can be certain who will suffer from some senseless act of bloodshed. And yet it goes on and on and on in this country of ours."

And it goes on at an increasing level. Of the 29 deadliest mass shootings in U.S. history, 19 have occurred since 2000.

That legislators lack the political will to take meaningful action against gun violence is mind-boggling. The Pew Research Center reported in 2023 that 4 in 10 Americans said they own a gun; a majority of those owners cited personal protection as one of the reasons. But in the same research, an equal number of Republican and Democratic respondents – 88 and 89 percent, respectively – said they support policies preventing people with mental illness from purchasing guns. And a majority – 69 percent Republicans, 90 percent Democrats – said they support increasing the minimum age for buying guns to 21.

The biggest threat to the Second Amendment is the abuse of it. Our constitutional rights require us to be responsible in our exercise of them. So why are we slow to act?

Two obstacles to action, perhaps:

One, dysfunction within our political system that has made it nearly impossible for lawmakers to work across the aisle to solve problems — even on issues on which both sides agree.

Two, a national soul that is becoming desensitized to gun violence. "... We seemingly tolerate a rising level of violence that ignores our common humanity and our claims to civilization alike," Robert Kennedy said in 1968. "We calmly accept newspaper reports of civilian slaughter in far off lands. We glorify killing on movie and television screens and call it entertainment. We make it easy for men of all shades of sanity to acquire weapons and ammunition they desire."

This collection of poetry acknowledges the pain suffered daily by so many of our fellow human beings. It is a prayer for comfort and healing. And it is a hope that we will, to paraphrase Tennyson, find the strength of will to strive, to seek, and to not yield in our pursuit of a safer, saner world.

— Richard Arlin Walker, editor

| PRESIDENT JOSEPH R. BIDEN JR.

Uvalde, Texas

(Adapted from President Biden's remarks to the nation on June 2, 2022)

Twenty-one crosses,
for 19 third- and fourth-graders
and two teachers.

On each cross, a name.

And nearby,
a photo of each victim.

Innocent victims

murdered in a classroom
that had been turned into
a killing field.

There are too many other schools,
too many other everyday places

that have become killing fields,

battlefields,

here in America.

Hundreds of family members
whose lives will never be the same
have one message for all of us:

Do something.

Just do something.

    For God's sake, do something.

The issue we face is one of
conscience
and common sense.

Over the last two decades,
more school-age children
have died from guns

than on-duty police officers and
active-duty military combined.

More kids than on-duty cops killed by guns.

More kids than soldiers killed by guns.

How much more carnage
are we willing to accept?

How many more innocent
American lives must
be taken before we say …

    Enough.

Imagine being that little girl,
that brave little girl in Uvalde

who smeared blood off her
murdered friend's body onto
her own face,

to lie still among the corpses
in her classroom and
pretend she was dead

in order to stay alive.

Enough.

Imagine what it would be
like for her to walk down
the hallway of any school again.

Enough.

Imagine what it's like for
children who experience this
kind of trauma every day

in school,

on the streets,

in communities
all across America.

Enough.

Imagine what it's like for
so many parents to hug
their children goodbye
in the morning,

not sure whether they'll
come back home.

Too many people don't have
to imagine that at all.

Enough.

It's time for each of us to do our part
for the children we've lost,

for the children we can save,
for the nation we love.

Let's hear the call and the cry.
Enough.

Let's meet the moment.
Enough.

Let us finally do something.
Enough.

What we will tell our children?

Sometimes the grandmother is not a grandmother but a wolf.
Sometimes the woodsman comes too late.

Sometimes the wolf's hunger is so great,
he eats his own heart, eats until he is nothing

but teeth and snap and rip. Sometimes
fur, bushy tail and an open-mouth smile means *pup*,

sometimes it doesn't,
and you know what can happen.
We can't protect you.

Usually the woodsman comes in time.
Usually the wolf passes the house.

Think of a face you love
    trace its lineaments in your mind,
    the arch of her cheek,
    the curve of his brow,
    how the lips part for a smile,
    purse for a kiss.

Recall the feelings you've seen
    play across the face you love:
    times of surprise,
    moments of pain,
    instances of love —
    looks given in love to you.
    Your face was loved then.
    The face you face daily,
    its wrinkles and worries,
    all the imperfections
    you've catalogued,
    was loved as it was,
    loved for the you within it,
    blessed by that face you love.

Remember when you saw the chin
    of that face you love
    on a stranger in a crowd?
    So similar it surprised you,
    brought that face you love to mind,
    how the hair or eye
    is shared in other faces,
    the lineaments you've loved

common to many,
arranged so variously,
each face like others

yet uniquely itself,
whole, and blessed.

For each face you see
has been loved
as you've been loved,
as you love
that face you love —
everyone,
everyone.

| JENNIFER (JENNY) COATES

Joker's Court

Shots ring out, nowhere to hide
inside music turned to madness, harmony
to dissonance.

If I were crazy, I could assume the ensuing
talk in Congress of silencers
to enhance a gunman's experience
was fake,

a parody of government, macabre
humour that bites the heart, so close to
truth, but luckily
untrue.

And yet, the Joker's Court here, unlike
Alice in Wonderland, is now real, and
I am not yet crazy.

| CATHY CUENIN

No going back

The radiance
of the harvest moon
is harsh
on our anguish
and there is no going back now

yet I want to turn
to earlier
before this full moon,
before the tragedy,
to change the rules,
the program
and layout,
the broken window,

to sit a while,
watch the waxing moon
grow fatter,
engage with the shooter

and to chat
— no,
not chat,
to listen
and then
listen some more.

Would I have heard?

Ten numbers

3,500,000 – 3668 – 1126 – 500 – 59 – 30 – 23 – 21 – 3.5 – 3 –1

3,500,000 — the amount of money donated by the NRA to current members of Congress *

3668 — the number of a bill in the House of Representatives that would reduce restrictions on silencers and armor piercing ammunition **

1226 — the number of miles from Las Vegas to Bainbridge Island, a distance shattered by the pain of one bullet ***

500 — the number people (roughly) who were injured in the Las Vegas shooting ****

30 – the number of people (at least) said to have been guided to safety by a man who was shot in the neck while helping them *****

23 — the number of guns the shooter in Las Vegas had with him ******

21 — the number of years since Congress cut funding for the Centers for Disease Control by the amount spent on researching gun violence as a public health issue *******

3.5 — the percentage by which the price of gun manufacturer Sturn Ruger's stock rose one day after the Las Vegas shooting ********

3 — the number of hours some people waited in line in Las Vegas to donate blood *********

1 — the percentage of people with serious mental illness who have perpetrated gun violence against strangers.**********

This simply does not compute.

* – Washington Post 10/2/2017
** – Congress.gov
*** – Google Maps
**** – NBCnews.com, 10/2/2017
***** – metro.co.uk, 10/03/2017
****** – NBCnews.com, 10/2/2017
******* – L.A. Times, 6/14/2016
******** – USA Today, 10/2/2017
********* – N.Y. Times.com, 10/2/2017
********** – Washington Post, 5/18/2016

| JOHN DAVIS

Jenny Parks, kindergarten teacher
In memoriam

What were her words before the bullets
entered her the way Hitler entered
Prague and bled the city dry?
In mid-song, between the drums and gunshots

and the singer's voice that twanged
like a flanged guitar in the Vegas night,
what were the last words that Jenny spoke?
Were they a fragment or complete sentence

and did her verb soothe like a smile
one that would urge kindergartners
to sit up, fold their hands into steeples,
open and watch all the people?

Please tell me. I am the substitute.
She left no lesson plans.
Her students are waiting
for the announcements

and the morning sing-along. Please tell me.
Ms. Parks will not be at school today.
Or tomorrow. Students will want me
to tell them what she said.

And how do I create a Jenny voice,

one that rattled and laughed
like rain on an aluminum roof?

| NEIL DOHERTY

Externality

*(Definition: An external effect, often unforeseen and unintended,
accompanying a process or activity)*

Who knows the reason that Fred got a gun,
was it protection or was it for fun?
He did not foresee, I will hazard a guess,
he'd snap in that moment of marital stress.

Gun in the cupboard but key in the door,
three-year-old Alice and five-year-old Shaw,
drawing and carefully taking his aim,
playing, pretending — it's only a game.

Three people slain when a man runs amok,
muscular Christian Conservative stock,
blowing through clinic and shooting at will,
deriding abortion and panning the pill.

Fourteen more killed in the west of L.A.
and yet we will read in the paper today
"guns do not kill" (it's recited by rote)—
kindly remember whenever you vote.

Fifty-nine more now in Vegas and yet
NRA lackies in Washington fret;
surely, they say, we dishonor this toll
should we even mention gun rights and control.

But 10-year-old Jason, Chicago south side,
nobody asked him how he would decide

and nobody will now, for what it is worth —
shot in the street in a tussle for turf.

| NEIL DOHERTY

Envoi

Happiness, liberty, life, are to be
sacrosanct only to lesser degree,
quite disregarded by setting our sights
on never constraining gun-ownership rights.

| CAROL DESPEAUX FAWCETT

In the ambulance

She lies in deep grass
under a tree of yellow cherries
sweet air of hibiscus
makes her sleepy

a canopy of faces
red lights paint the sky
her heart stops

a stranger leans in
lips sweet and hopeful
as yellow cherries

When the world is spinning, I remember
these are my loves: red wine,
orange cats, the smell of clove cigarettes,
Leonard Cohen's gravelly voice,
words like *sibilate* and *firefly* and *lovely* and *valium*,

rain like pebbles on my sunroom roof,
or hail the size of Easter eggs,
church bells in the morning,
cradling my guitar like a tired friend,
leaning into corners on my motorcycle,

an unquenchable thirst for love and laughter,
a hunger that isn't hunger but a life
reaching back for itself, singing too loudly,
swimming in the ocean,
warm water like lips sliding over my skin,

the water in me searching for the water not in me,
my body like sand consuming the tides.

A gamble of red
Spilled spirits soaring
Opposite of the bet

| BEV HANSON

The ghost man of Mandalay

On a mission of fun my daughter and her husband checked in.
On a mission of death the ghost man checked in on the very
same day.

On Floor 33 my daughter and her husband went to their room.
Just below on Floor 32 the ghost man entered his room.

On Floor 33 my daughter and her husband peered out the
window. They saw a festival of happy people.
On Floor 32 the ghost man peered out with the very same view.

He saw a gathering of targets.

At 5 p.m. on that awful day my daughter and her husband
left for the airport.
At 5 p.m. on that awful day the ghost man stayed to do what
he meant to do.

My daughter and her husband came home.
The ghost man didn't go home,
and neither did so very many.

Why?

| **GOV. JAY INSLEE**

(*Adapted from remarks made by Gov. Inslee of Washington on Oct. 3, 2017 after the mass shooting in Las Vegas, Nevada*)

Once again,
we are mourning
the violent loss of innocent lives

to a man who had access to
weapons no civilian should
have access to.

It's impossible to know how to stop
every act of gun violence,

but I know with my whole being
that our nation's leaders
aren't even trying.

| ANNE KUNDTZ

When is a water droplet home ...
Pelting its beads onto agave's broad leaves
to drip deep into aquifer, to acequia, to ocean
each drop a ballet battement across shallow ponds,
to rise en pointe before settling?

Or is a water droplet home
rising in the desert sun, called to hazy blue sky,
cirrus, cumulus, cumulonimbus,
those giant flat-bottomed thunderheads?

Where does a soul find home
when bullets rain down into a neon ocean
of people, once clapping, swaying waves of music —
and now lying flat, trembling, a turbulent sea
as bullets ping across the seats, ricochet through the terror.

Where does a soul find home?
In the restless aftermath
souls rise above the screams,
leave long black bags of hurt and anger
for loved ones and survivors to carry.

Souls gather in thin wisps
as we pick up prickly shards,
as we begin to heal this desert home.

| DIANE LEE MOSER

Message from Las Vegas

They rained from the sky
no address ...
mixed messages
from a mixed mind.

Second Amendment
opened the door
insanity stepped through
held bodies in its hand.

Now our Nation cries out
for the innocent,
the broken hearts,
The Future ...

| NANCY REKOW

That afternoon the war ended

we picked every green tomato in the garden,
dipped them in flour,
fried them for supper,
and nobody
argued over the dishes.

Hours we ran through the sprinkler
leaping like salmon to its wet circular hiss,
shooting each other over and over with the hose,
flopping on the grass, gasping,
air heavy with Mother's peonies.

It was any summer night.
There the big dipper hung.
Up on the porch, dozens of papery moths
blundered against the light
and fell with no sound.

| ALIONA ROMAN

The world didn't seem to stop to me,
even as my mother blared CNN from our living room
on the second of October,

I couldn't feel feelings for hours.
Nothing but numbness, while hours before
hundreds felt confusion and fear.

The world stopped turning for them,
for the mothers and fathers,
husbands and wives, brothers and sisters

it was a bang, cut off by screams
of concert goers that were heard throughout
the streets of Sin City that night.

The world continued that morning.
It was with silence
that consumes everything.

Numb and still,
my world continued to turn.

Fates are shuffling
like a deck of cards
in a child's hands

Unlit matches
stacked up against
gasoline cans

I wish the moon a magnet
strong enough to suck
the bullets out

I say goodbye too long.
I look them in the eyes and hold on
so tight I break my heart bones.

The what ifs are unbearable.

What if they don't come home?
There is a shooter in the classroom
firing bullets into our babies.

What if they are swallowed
by a hurricane and die choking,
My name on their lips?

What if they are scorched,
charcoaled into ashes
by wildfire?

What if they hang themselves
in the school bathroom
to prove a bully wrong, or right?

What if they take or are slipped
a bathroom cabinet pharmaceutical
that gets them high forever?

What if they go to hear their favorite
singer with their favorite friends and
they all get gunned down dancing?

What if they don't come home?
There is a shooter in the classroom
firing bullets into our babies.

I say goodbye too long.
I look them in the eyes and hold on
so tight I break my heart bones.

The what ifs are unbearable.

| SHARON E. SVENDSEN

About my feet ...
Yes, they're called feet.

Metric feet, the accents
in lines of poems.

"Kaboom Kaboom" is two iambic feet.

"Ta ta tum, ta ta tum" is two
anapestic feet.

May my feet walk toward mercy.

May my feet walk toward peace.

May my feet walk toward reason,
reason and truth,

and

May my feet kick away
(in words)
at anger, torture, murder.

May my footprints overflow
To a better world.

Waxing harvest moon
Blood red in a smoky sky
Reflecting the lost.

| DIANE WALKER

A couplet

What choice have we, when dealing with such horror
and such grief,
but to insist that we take steps to end this slaughter?

| DIANE WALKER

A haiku

Echoes of gunshots
shimmer above the desert;
warblers fall silent.

Scarlet pillows
seeping
hemorrhaging
spreading

like a stain
Our great stain
nothing removes

Lady MacBeth
has nothing on us

An answer?
Any answer?
Stoicism
Acceptance of pain
and suffering.

Wherever it happens ...
it doesn't stay there.

Joseph R. Biden Jr. is the 46th president of the United States. He served as the nation's 47th vice president from 2009-2017, as U.S. senator from Delaware from 1973-2009, and as a New Castle County Council member from 1971-73. As president, he signed into law the Bipartisan Safer Communities Act, which extends background checks for gun purchasers younger than 21, clarifies federal firearms license requirements, provides funding for state red flag laws and other crisis intervention programs, further criminalizes arms trafficking, and partially closes loopholes through which abusive partners formerly could obtain firearms.

Michele Bombardier's collection, "What We Do," was a finalist for the Washington Book Award. Her poetry and book reviews can be found in dozens of literary journals such as *JAMA*, *Alaska Quarterly Review*, *Atlanta Review*, *Parabola*, *Bellevue Literary Review*, and many others. She holds an MFA in poetry from Pacific University. She is the founder of Fishplate Poetry, offering workshops, editing and retreats while raising funds for humanitarian relief.

Kent Chadwick's poetry has appeared in the *Floating Bridge Review*, *World Haiku Review*, *Be Which*, *The Bainbridge Islander*, *Exhibition*, *Switched-on Gutenberg*, *The Raven Chronicles*, *Left Bank*, *Sojourners*, the chapbooks *The Jack Straw Writers Program 1999* and *Fishtrap Anthology V*, and the anthology *Deep Down Things: Poems of the Inland Pacific Northwest*. *He is the author of* "God comes to us like a caterpillar: Jesus' stories retold for kids" and "A Balance of Shadows: Gregg Chadwick's Paintings" (Wisdom Press).

Jennifer (Jenny) Coates' poems have been published in several anthologies and collections. She served as co-executive director of Arts & Humanities Bainbridge and is a tax and business law attorney.

Cathy Cuenin (1949-2022) was a tugboat owner, painter, writer, and retired nurse. She lived for 17 years after a lung transplant and authored the book, "The Way I Walk, from Tugboat to Transplant."

Marsha Cutting is a retired psychologist who sails, advocates for those with disabilities, and is involved in anti-racism and environmental work.

John Davis is the author of two collections of poetry, "The Reservist" (2005) and "Gigs" (2011). His work has been published in *DMQ Review, Iron Horse Literary Review, One,* and *Rio Grande Review*. He teaches high school and performs in blues bands.

Neil Doherty, a retired professor from the Wharton School of Economics with many articles and technical books to his credit, now lives on Bainbridge Island. When Donald Trump won the presidential election in 2016, Doherty turned to poetry to help him work through his disappointment. The outcome is his chapbook "A Treasury of Trump" (2017).

Carol Despeaux Fawcett is an award-winning poet whose work has appeared in many journals. Her book of poetry, "The Dragon & The Dragonfly" (Blue Dragonfly Press), is an accumulation of her 35-year love affair with poetry. She is a past winner of the Pacific Northwest Writers Contest for memoir and poetry, and a finalist in the Writer's Digest Annual Poetry Competition and the Surrey International Writers' Conference. She earned her MFA from Goddard College.

Amy K. Genova's poems appear in *3Elements*, *Cold Lake Anthology*, *Cream City Review*, *Ghost City Press*, *The R.E.A.L.*, *Flying Island*, *Homestead Review*, *The Thieving Magpie*, and others. Her ekphrastic poems show in galleries beside representative artwork; "A Life in Yellow – Redux," was chosen for a juried show. Her memoir, "Moving," was published in *Stonecrop*.

Bev Hanson's creative outlet focused solely on digital art and photography until she became the coordinator for Ars Poetica (art and poetry combination) in Kitsap County for two years. She ventured into writing poetry with the encouragement of poet and publisher Nancy Rekow, and now enjoys the written word as well as illustration.

Jay Inslee is the 23rd governor of Washington. He served in the U.S. House of Representatives from 1993-95 and 1999-2012, and in the Washington state House of Representatives from 1989-1993. He lives on Bainbridge Island.

Anne Kundtz writes with her students in Creative Writing and sophomore English on Bainbridge Island. Her poems have been published in *Writing All Morning*, *Ars Poetica*, *Poetry Corners*, *Mountain Mail* and other print and online publications.

Diane Lee Moser has written poems all her life and began sharing them in the mid-2010s. She's been a social worker, crisis counselor, bookkeeper and traveler, and started a food bank on Bainbridge Island.

Nancy Rekow (1932-2023) was an award-winning poet, writing teacher, editor and publisher. She was the catalyst for *Island of Geese and Stars* and *The Northwest Poets and Artists Calendar*, and collaborated for several years on the publication of *Ars Poetica*.

She was the first director of the Bainbridge Island Arts Council (now Arts & Humanities Bainbridge), and organized poetry readings at Bainbridge's San Carlos Restaurant and Poulsbo's Poulsbohemian Coffeehouse.

Aliona Roman studied creative writing in Anne Kundst's Creative Writing class at Bainbridge High School and contributed to "Poems for Las Vegas" (2017, Kitsap Publishing).

Tamera Roza has a lifelong passion for poetry but finds all forms of writing gratifying and cathartic. "In making and sharing art, we heal and grow," she said.

Sharon E. Svendsen's fiction, articles and more than 200 poems have been published in many literary magazines, periodicals and anthologies. Among them: *Plainsongs, Rat's Ass Review, Feathertale #15 and #16, Spank the Carp, Decasp, Poetry Corners,* and *Ars Poetica.* She has a BA in English with a Creative Writing emphasis from the University of Washington.

Val Tollefsen is a retired trial lawyer and former mayor of Bainbridge Island. He has often found peace and meaning in the poetry of others and is honored to have made a 17-syllable contribution to this healing gesture.

Diane Walker is a contemplative photographer, painter, playwright, and poet who produces a daily blog of poems and photos (www.facebook.com/contemplativephotography). A former Seattle marketing executive, Walker lives on Bainbridge Island and serves as volunteer station manager for Bainbridge Community Broadcasting.

Jeff Wenker is a writer and winemaker. He worked in the Barossa Valley, South Australia, a region featured in his novel, "The Russian Books"; and completed a vintage at Siduri Winery in Santa Rosa, California, a place also traumatized by tragedy, which is featured in his novel, "Mad Crush."

The editor of this book, **Richard Arlin Walker,** is a journalist and mariner living in Anacortes, Washington. He is the author of two books of local history ("Roche Harbor", "Point No Point") and two books of poetry ("The Journey Home" and "Frybread Dreams & Other Poems"); and co-author of a reference book ("Indian Country Stylebook for Editors, Writers and Journalists").

| ALSO FROM DEER DANCER PRESS

Indian Country Stylebook for Editors, Writers and Journalists

Frybread Dreams & Other Poems

The Cedar Tree | A Journal

www.ingramcontent.com/pod-product-compliance
Lightning Source LLC
Chambersburg PA
CBHW051648250726
48653CB00007B/2553